A Passionat

A play

Kay Mellor

Samuel French — London
New York - Toronto - Hollywood

Please see page iv for further copyright information

A PASSIONATE WOMAN

First performed at the Courtyard Theatre, West Yorkshire Playhouse, Leeds, on 5th May, 1993 with the following cast:

Betty	Anne Reid
Mark	Derek Hicks
Craze	Gary Mavers
Donald	David Hargreaves

Directed by David Liddiment
Décor by Di Seymour
Lighting by Greg Turbyne
Sound by Mic Pool

Subsequently performed at the Comedy Theatre, London, on 7th November, 1994, with the following cast:

Betty	Stephanie Cole
Mark	Neil Morrissey
Craze	James Gaddas
Donald	Alfred Lynch

Directed by Ned Sherrin
Décor by Patrick Connellan
Lighting by Alan Burrett
Sound by Matthew Eagland

CHARACTERS

Betty
Mark
Craze
Donald

Jo (non-speaking)
Various off stage voices

Scene — the loft and roof top of a pre-war house in the
   suburbs of Leeds

Time — 1993

ACT I   Saturday morning, 10 a.m.

ACT II   Twenty minutes later

AUTHOR'S NOTE

A speech usually follows the one immediately before it but when one character starts speaking before the other has finished, the point of interruption has been marked with a / thereby giving an overlapping effect. For example:

Mark Aunty Margaret'll do your hair / and you'll look great.
Craze You're beautiful.

Craze starts speaking after Mark has said "hair".

K.M.

A NOTE ON STAGING

Set details in this text represent the author's original intentions for the production of the play at the Comedy Theatre in the West End, which used a revolve. Amateur groups who do not have the resources to achieve this staging may find the following suggestions helpful:

For stages without trap-doors, build up the set and create one, or use an entrance at the side; Betty can push items *against* a door, rather than placing them *over* one.

The attic and external roof can be seen side by side, with a chimney L for Betty to hide behind in Act II, until she appears when Mark sticks his head though the skylight (page 37). Although the playing space will be tight in this roof "half", all the necessary effects can be accomplished provided that a strong framework has been built to support the main setting. The ladder which Donald climbs up can appear at point A. Craze can walk along B to C. Mark can slip from the skylight to the gutter D. For the stage direction *Mark moves effortlessly up the roof as though being pulled by some supernatural force*, an inconspicuous nylon rope with a clip strategically placed at the end should run down one of the vertical slate grooves in the roof. The actor playing Mark should, after free-falling down to the projected gutter, attach the awaiting clip to his body harness at the point of the split in his morning suit tails, thereby enabling the stage crew behind the roof area to either winch or simply pull Mark up the roof. The fire brigade hoist can truck on at E and, with a minimum of "flying" space, a hot air balloon *basket* and bottom end of the coloured silk can appear above the roof. (At this point, Betty's line "I don't believe it" [Page 51] can read "I don't believe it. It's a balloon!") A small platform can be built behind the roof section, on which Donald and Betty stand before she flies off. A tightening pin spot on Betty, with a darkened surround, can also add to the effect of her "leaving" the stage.

The publishers would be pleased to hear of other staging suggestions.

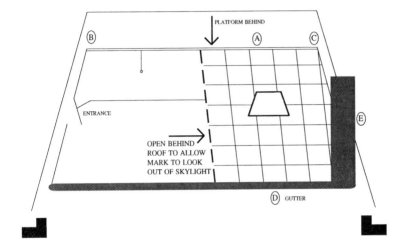

ACT I

1993. Saturday morning, 10.00 a.m.

The loft of a pre-war house in the suburbs of Leeds

A centre beam runs across the roof of the loft and two supporting smaller beams are to either side. The roof slopes down towards the back of the stage. To the R there is a skylight window which looks rather dusty, but a small amount of daylight filters through on to the water-tank underneath. An electric light bulb hangs from a piece of wire; it has been rigged in rather a makeshift way. The light switch hangs from the centre beam on a piece of brown cord. Just off C is the opening to the loft; a three-foot-square wooden flap

The loft is full of various discarded items: an artificial Christmas tree; a box of baubles and old Christmas cards tied up; a brown carrier-bag full of old Christmas cards; used tins of paint stacked on top of an old-fashioned heavy record-player; a box of old LPs; a rolled-up carpet; a lilac wooden high-chair with multi-coloured baubles painted on the tray; parts of a baby's wooden cot; three battered suitcases, including one large, brown one containing clothes, etc.; four dining room-chairs stacked seat to seat near the skylight; a cabinet covered in papers; a trunk; loose rolls of linoleum

The flap suddenly moves, as though someone has banged it from below. Light from the landing streams up, illuminating the head of a sweeping broom poking its nose into the loft space. Then the broom disappears, leaving the flap misplaced. From below we hear the sound of several heavy books being placed one on top of another. A short pause, then we hear someone puffing and panting. The sweeping broom comes hurtling through into the attic with some force. It lands on the loft floor. The flap moves completely to one side and two hands appear

Betty, a middle-aged, homely sort of woman, levers herself up in a rather ungainly manner and manages to get one of her feet on to the frame. As she heaves herself up into the loft, we see she has a lovely face, but her figure is slightly on the plump side. Her hair is set in rather stiff curls around her face and she wears an expensively tailored, dusky pink, two-piece suit, with a navy hat and accessories. Over the top of the suit she wears a brown-checked nylon overall. She catches her leg on the opening, inspects her tights, tuts, stands upright, looks about the attic and tuts again. She goes over to the brown cord light switch, and switches it on. There is light

Betty I've been to the new Asda. It's really nicely laid out. Our Mark took me last Saturday in his new car ... (*Her eyes fall upon the old wooden baby's high-chair*) It's not brand new, it's new to him, it's very smooth, you can hardly hear it going ... (*She goes over to the high-chair*) He saved up. I wanted us to give him something towards it, but Donald doesn't hold with that, says they have no appreciation of money ... (*she runs her hands along the high chair with great tenderness*) says they have to fend for themselves in this life, says they grow up lazy, says I spoil him anyway. He's just tight really ... (*She decides not to go on with this line of conversation and starts to tidy up*) Anyway don't ask me what it is, 'cos I'm hopeless with cars, it's blue and it's got a boot. I'd asked him a few times to take me, 'cos it's not easy to get to on the bus and they've got bumper bags of cat litter on offer, but you have to catch the number one and it goes right round the ring road and then you've got a five-minute walk at the other end and then you've got it all to do on the way back. (*She drops a tin of paint on the floor. She stands motionless for a moment waiting, then*) It's all right for them that live on the number thirty-six, or thirty-three route, but it's a bit of a drawback for us at this side, still they have a very nice cheese counter, they had cheeses I've never even heard of ...

We hear a man's voice

Donald (*off*) Betty!

Betty stands motionless for a couple of seconds, then tiptoes across the floor, kneels down and quietly puts the flap back over the opening. She waits for another second, then stands and carries on tidying up on tiptoe. Occasionally she looks out to the audience, but her gaze is always focused to a particular spot, as though she is speaking to one person at a time

Betty (*quietly*) No, I had no idea there was so many cheeses and the girls behind the counter ... they wear these funny little hats, like a trilby with a net at the back, I think they're supposed to keep their hair back, but they just plonk them on their heads, one of them had it hung all over her face, they'd be better with a pony tail or a nice plait ... (*she forgets what she was saying*) anyway if you ask them, they'll give you a bit to taste. I had some of that blue stuff, Donald says that's where the maggots have crawled through, I just had a little bit, I think it's an acquired taste really. I have to be careful with cheese though, because I tend to put weight on with it. I never used to have a problem, I was a size twelve till I was forty-three, except when I had our Mark, but six months after, I'd be back into my size twelves. I know plenty of women who've had to buy a complete new wardrobe. Our Margaret, me sister, was a size sixteen for years after she had her first, Graham. Mind you that's our Margaret all over, any excuse for a new frock, she's always got what she wanted ... and then she had to go into hospital and have it all taken away ——

Donald (*off; concerned, agitated, louder*) Betty! Are you there? Will you answer me.

Betty waits for a minute then pulls a couple of the suitcases, etc. over the opening to secure it down

Betty — she went dead thin, she had to have *another* whole new wardrobe, it's a good job she wasn't married to Donald, that's all I can say. Mind you that was when it all started, when she got her figure back, she upped and left Eric, that was her husband, and she took little Graham with her, I mean he was only six, bless him, I blame that for him starting to stammer. He's had speech therapy and everything, it's awful, you want to finish his sentences off for him. I have to bite me tongue. I never took to Eric. He had squiffy eyes, now there's nothing wrong with that. I mean he couldn't help it, but you were never quite sure if he were talking to you or the person stood next to you, it was very confusing, still he was good to our Margaret, he married her and he'd no need to, 'cos there was a bit of a kerfuffle at the time, but as soon as Graham was born, it was clear he was Eric's, he's got the same squint, when I used to look at the pair of them together I'd go all dizzy. It's a shame really. Well, she's on her fourth now, husband that is, he's called Mal ... Mal ... what kind of name is that? He's thirty-seven, now I'm not saying anything, but she tells people she's forty-two, I tell her "No, Margaret, you're getting confused, that's the year you were born", she doesn't like it, but I think she needs telling. I'll tell you what though, do you know what he bought her for her fiftieth? A balloon ride, we were all there, the whole family, Kettlewell, in a field. Off she went like the girl in the Nimble advert, screaming and hanging on to ... Mal ... for dear life, I said to Donald, now that's romantic, but he thought it was a waste of money, "What have they got at the end of it," he says. I said it's an experience Donald, they've got their memories, but he doesn't understand ... You should have seen her climbing into that basket, she was showing all her stocking tops, but she didn't care. She was the first to wear seamless you know, I said, "Margaret, you look like you've got nothing on your legs". She said, "Betty! Life's complicated enough without having to worry about straight seams". I thought, "Yes, some people make their own complications, Margaret", but I didn't say it ... She spends a fortune on herself, you name it she's had it, or she's off out to get it. You should see her ... thirty-seven ... she's asking for trouble.

There is banging on the flap and the suitcases move about. Betty looks alarmed — she didn't expect Donald to find her so quickly. She goes and sits on the cases

Mind, there are advantages to being heavy.

Mark (*off*) Mam!

Betty (*surprised*) It's our Mark.

Mark I know you're up there! Mam? Will you answer me?

Betty No!

Mark (*off*) I want to talk to you!

Betty That's our Mark.

Mark (*off*) What are you doing up there?

Beat

(*Off*) Talk to me will you?

Beat

(*Off*) Mother!

Betty Go away!

Mark (*off*) Please! ... Mam?

Betty moves the suitcases off the flap and Mark levers himself up into the loft. Mark is aged thirty-one. He is a handsome, confident man, dressed in a light-grey morning suit and pink cravat. He struggles to get up inside

Betty Mind your back ... (*She holds her hand out to help him up*) It's the easiest thing in the world to crick your back. When I was pregnant with you, I was cutting your nanna's hair and ——

Mark Mother! / What are you doing up here?

Betty I don't like "Mother", I hate "Mother". You know I don't like it.

Mark What are you doing up here?

Betty I was telling you about my back, aren't you interested?

Mark Of course I want to hear / about your ——

Betty You don't, you're only interested in yourself.

Mark Mum! / I'm supposed to be ——

Betty How did you know where I was?

Mark Two volumes of the *Encyclopaedia Britannica* and *The Modern Women's Medical Guide* on top of landing cupboard. You could have hurt yourself.

Betty I know what I'm doing, which is more than you do. You could have seriously hurt yourself the way you pulled yourself up here. Backs are a real problem you know, you have to look after them, once they go, that's it, you'll have trouble all your life, vertebraes popping out all over the place. You have to bend your knees, let them take the strain, I know because that woman from the welfare told me how to lift your nanna. Has your father gone for her?

Mark You know she won't get in me dad's car without you being there.

Betty She'll think we're not coming.

Mark Dad's going berserk looking for you.

Betty Let him.

Mark That's not very nice is it? I mean you went upstairs ... (*he looks at his watch*) nearly half an hour ago to put a spare toilet roll in the bathroom and you disappeared off the face of this earth. He's worried. He's gone down to the shops to see if you're there ...

Betty Well, he'll be disappointed, won't he? (*She puts the lid securely back on the flap and goes to lift the paint tins off the old record-player*)

Mark What are you doing?

Betty Tidying up.

Mark (*exasperated*) Oh God! I'm getting married in an hour and thirty-five minutes and my mother's in the loft, checking out cobwebs, I can't believe this.

Betty bends her knees as she tries to lift the record-player

Will you stop doing that. What are you trying to do?

Betty (*starting to walk the gramophone player over towards the flap*) It's all right, I can manage. I want it over there.

Mark Where?

Betty On top of the flap.

Mark stands in front of her to stop her moving the record-player any further. She puts it down. (The record-player remains "plugged in", so the cord should disappear off towards a wall)

Mark I can't cope with this. Mother, will you stop / that and listen to me ——

Betty There's that "Mother" again.
Mark We've got to go down now.

Betty stares at him, then looks down at her tights

Betty I knew they'd run.
Mark We'll buy you some more.
Betty I've got another pair in my drawer, I got them at the Asda, I said I'd better get an extra pair / just in case, don't you remember?
Mark Yes, right, fine, let's go down and then you can find them.
Betty I was telling you something.
Mark (*putting his arm round her and coaxing her away from the gramophone player*) I heard you, you were cutting me nan's hair. You can tell me on the way / down.
Betty No!
Mark (*taking his arm away from her*) Why not?

She turns away from him

For God's sake!!!
Betty You've no need to blaspheme!
Mark I'm sorry, but I'm a bit tense this morning. I think that's understandable. This happens to be the most important day of my life, the day I've been waiting for, for nearly eighteen months and I want things to run smoothly, that's all, so I'm sorry that I blasphemed ——
Betty And you raised your voice ...
Mark —— and I'm sorry for raising my voice. I'm really really sorry, but can we please just go downstairs? ... *Please*, Mum? ... For me?

Beat

Betty I was cutting your nanna's hair, just trimming it at the back. You know how she always likes me to do her hair, well I must have been about four months' pregnant with you, but I wasn't showing, I carried very neat. I had my yellow fitted dress on, I just leant over so I could get to the hairs on the back of her neck and that was it — it locked. I was doubled up. They had to send for an ambulance. They prodded me about and then I felt something give, like an elastic band and the pain went just like that. The doctor said my stomach muscles were so strong they wouldn't let the baby grow, fancy that.
Mark Have you finished now?
Betty And thirty-one years later they stand arguing with you in your loft and your stomach muscles are knackered.

Mark Mum!
Betty What?
Mark That's swearing.
Betty I might like to swear.
Mark What's the matter with you?
Betty You swear, I've heard you.
Mark Not in front of you I don't.
Betty Well I feel like swearing today. I might even say the "f" word, you never know.
Mark What's got into you. What's wrong?

Beat — no answer

All right, if you feel like swearing, swear. Go on say it.
Betty I'm saving it up for later.
Mark Later when?
Betty Later on.
Mark Well let me know won't you 'cos I'd like me future mother-in-law out of earshot when you do.
Betty Don't worry, I won't embarrass you.
Mark Good ... Look, they'll be all here soon, cars and everything. Come on Mum, this is me you're talking to.
Betty For the last time, eh?
Mark What?
Betty For the last time we'll be talking together.
Mark Y'what?
Betty Well we won't be able to have our little chats anymore.
Mark Course we will.
Betty No. After today, it'll be all / different ——
Mark It's a bit of paper, Mam, that's all it is.
Betty — you'll talk to her now instead.
Mark Mam! ... I can talk to both of you ... Come on. Flowers have come. We've got a lovely spray for your suit.
Betty I'm not a child, Mark.
Mark Well what the bloody hell are you doing up here then?
Betty I prefer it.
Mark You can sit up here all day after the wedding, every day, as much as you like. In fact you can move up here.
Betty It wouldn't bother you would it?
Mark Mam, I just need to get through today with as least hassle as possible. That's all I want. It's not much to ask.
Betty It doesn't pay you in the end you know.

Mark What?
Donald (*off*) Betty!
Mark He's back.
Donald (*off*) Mark! She's not there! Mark!

Betty puts her hand over Mark's mouth

(*Off*) Where's he gone now?

Mark takes his mother's hand away

Mark I don't understand why you're doing this? Are you trying to deliberately hurt him?
Betty How is me being up here hurting him?
Mark He doesn't know where you are.
Betty I'm here.
Mark But he doesn't know that, does he? I mean you could be under a bus, for all he knows.
Betty The house is tidy.
Mark What's that got to do with it?
Betty The spare bed's made up in case anyone wants to sleep, I suppose our Margaret and Mal'll want a bed, that's if she's still with him.
Mark They'll be here soon. Everybody'll be here soon.
Betty I've baked enough pies to last a year and they're all wrapped and dated in the freezer.
Mark He'll see the books.
Betty I've polished the furniture and cleaned the brasses.
Mark You're going to have to come down sometime, Mum.
Betty I've done the steps ...
Mark Good ...
Betty Mopped the kitchen floor ...
Mark Wonderful ...
Betty Vac'd the carpets ...
Mark Right ...
Betty Harpic-ed the toilet ...
Mark Yeh ...
Betty Washed and ironed the clothes ...
Mark Yep.
Betty Packed your suitcase ...
Mark Thanks ...
Betty Watered the plants ...
Mark What are you trying to say, Mum?

Betty Put the spare toilet roll in the bathroom ...
Mark You don't have to do all that you know ...
Betty Cleaned the windows ...
Mark Mam!
Betty Emptied the rubbish ...
Mark Mam!!
Betty Fed the fish ...
Mark Mam!!!
Betty (*shouting at him*) What am I supposed to do now?

Beat. Mark doesn't know what to say

Mark I don't know what you ... Anything you want I suppose ... you can do anything you like now.
Betty (*taking her hat pin out of her hat*) I don't want to do nothing. (*She takes her hat off*) I'm staying here.
Mark You're not! You're coming to my wedding.
Betty (*setting about tidying up again*) Did you ever see such a mess?
Mark You can't stop up here, you're talking ridiculous, what's up with you? ... Come on? ... Tell me.
Betty It's filthy.
Mark It doesn't matter. Nobody comes up here!
Betty I do! I come up here. Me. Betty Derbyshire, née Wilson. This is my place.
Mark All right!
Betty Well then.
Mark Listen Mum, I know this is about Jo, I know you don't like her / but I——
Betty I do like her, I never said anything about not liking her.

Mark looks at her

All right, she's not what I'd've picked for you, / but ——
Mark You always say that, no matter who it is, I could have brought Lady Diana home / and you'd have said she wasn't right for me.
Betty (*correcting him*) Princess Diana. (*Of Charles*) Well, she obviously wasn't right for him either.
Mark Well I'm sorry, Mam, but I like Jo, she makes me happy, I don't care if she's not what you'd have picked for me. I'm not asking you to pick for me, I don't want you to pick for me. I can pick for meself.
Betty (*ignoring him*) And Andrew, he couldn't pick either.
Mark I'm marrying Jo.

Betty Or Anne, she couldn't pick either ... She's stand-offish.

Mark Well her mother is the Queen of England.

Betty I mean Jo.

Mark Jo! She's not stand-offish at all, she's just a bit shy, she's tried her best to ... make you like her.

Beat

I can't stay at home forever, Mam.

Betty I didn't ask you to.

Mark Well then.

Betty I don't want you to.

Mark Good, as long as we've got that straight.

Beat

Betty I just don't know why you're rushing.

Mark Rushing? I'm not rushing. I'm thirty-one, I'll be thirty-two in a couple of months, that's hardly rushing.

Betty You've only known her two minutes.

Mark Eighteen months.

Betty Why don't you get engaged, most people get engaged, our Graham got engaged.

Mark At nineteen he got engaged, Mam. He's married with two children now and he's younger than me.

Betty Well he was lucky to get someone wasn't he, with all his problems. It must have taken him a good hour for him to spit the proposal out and he was probably asking her friend anyway.

Mark (*shocked*) Mother!

Betty (*apologetically*) Well.

Mark Do you realize that every single one of my friends are married or have been married, some of them are on their second ——

Betty Well that's because they rushed the first.

Mark I'm the last one.

Betty There's nothing wrong with that.

Mark I can't live at home for ever.

A moment passes

Betty She won't let them call her nanna you know, your Aunty Margaret, they call her Maggie. It's 'cos she's with him. She won't baby-sit either, I think it's awful. Young ones need time of their own. I expect she's too busy having sexual shenanigans with "Mal". She's self, self, self is our Margaret and so is Jo.

Mark No she isn't. You're wrong.

Betty She bosses you about.

Mark That's just her way.

Betty I don't like to see you being bossed about.

Mark I love her, Mum.

Pause

Betty She's very pretty I'll give you that, although she spoils herself wearing those big ear-rings and black boots and she can't cook, I mean what happens when you start with a family? Oh! I forgot she doesn't want children.

Mark has been through this before

Mark She does, not yet that's all, she's got her career to think of.

Betty I don't even know what software is.

Mark She writes programs for computers.

Betty Programmes! It's all programmes these days. I see enough programmes that your father has on the box. He sits glued to that screen from morning till night. He watches this programme and that programme. If I put the wireless on he tuts, "I can't hear the programme," he says, so I just get on with some housework ...

Mark Mam! Jo's not like that. She's clever, she makes me laugh, I love her and she loves me and that's all there is to it.

Betty Well I hope you'll both be very happy.

Pause

Mark You always knew that one day I'd get married.

Betty You used to say, "I'll never leave, I'll always be there for you".

Mark I will always be there for you.

Betty Well, why Nottingham then?

Mark Because that's where Jo's contract is and she earns more than I do and I can get a job anywhere.

Betty She must have applied to Nottingham.

Mark I suppose she must have.

Betty Well I think that's terrible. What about her mum?

Mark She's pleased for her, pleased that she's got a job, pleased she's happy, / pleased she'll be ——

Betty All those years she spent bringing her up and that's how she repays
her ...

Mark Repays her for what? Giving birth to her, feeding her, what are you
talking about?

Betty I'm talking about the years of life that you give up for your children.

Mark Give up? Who asks you to give anything up? Nobody! You decide to
have a child, nobody forces you, nobody says ——

Betty You've no idea what you're talking about, wait till you've got children
of your own.

Mark I thought the whole point of having children was to make your life
richer not poorer.

Betty You don't know anything.

Mark All right, what did you give up for me? Come on, I want to know?

Beat

Betty I could never have left your nanna ——

Mark You're changing the subject.

Betty — I'd have been too worried about her ...

Mark I'm talking about me and you.

Betty Your Aunty Margaret never even told me mother when she ran off to
Kirby Overblow. It was up to me as usual. All Margaret was bothered about
was her precious gas man.

Mark We aren't running off / to some ——

Betty She wants to have you all to herself.

Mark No she doesn't, you've got her all wrong. She's got a year's contract
and then we don't know what we're doing, we might come back, we might
go on somewhere else. I'll never lose touch with you. I'll always see you
and now Dad's retired, you can come and stay with us, have a little holiday.

Betty In Nottingham?

Mark It's two hours away, if that.

Betty Your Aunty Margaret said we could stay with her in Kirby Overblow,
but when we went they were never in.

Mark Well we will be. Anyway you can ring first.

Betty For an invitation.

Mark To make sure we're in.

Betty It'll always be "we" now, won't it? You and Jo, Jo and Mark. "Us" 'll
be you and her. You'll lose yourself Mark, you'll lose who you are.

Mark I'm marrying her, Mum.

Betty Well go on then, I'm not stopping you. Go and get married to her.

Mark You are stopping me, Mam, because you're up here and you should
be downstairs. I know why you're doing this, but it won't work I'm telling

you, so you can forget it now, this is just silly. You've had your hair done, you've bought yourself a new suit, you've been cleaning the house up for a fortnight.

Betty (*starting to busy herself again, moving old pieces of lino about*) And now I'm cleaning up here.

Mark What the hell for?!

Betty (*finding an old LP*) Because I want to! Whatever happened to Clodagh Rodgers?

Mark I've no bloody idea.

Betty (*staring at him*) I didn't bring you up to be foul-mouthed.

She starts to move some old papers off a cabinet to make room for the roll of lino. Mark sees that the back of Betty's skirt is dirty

Mark You're getting your suit all dirty.

Betty I don't care, I don't like it anyway, it's too tight, it wrinkles up round me middle. The saleswoman said it'd help me diet, but I knew it wouldn't. It's not me anyway. I'm not a dusky pink sort of person.

Mark Don't do this to me, Mum.

Betty I'm not doing anything ... (*Giving him the roll of lino*) Hold that, will you. Your father insists on keeping the off-cuts, I don't know what he thinks we're going to do with them. They just clutter the place up. Half of this stuff is ——

Mark I've got to go down, Mum.

Betty Why?

Mark (*exasperated*) Because I'm getting married! We've got to be setting off soon ...

Betty But not for a bit yet ...

Pause as Betty and Mark communicate silently to one another. Mark sees the hurt in his mother's eyes. She diverts her attention to a large old battered brown suitcase

Betty Do you know that case has been everywhere with us, Mablethorpe, Filey, Llandudno, every holiday we went on, the big brown case'd come out ...

Mark Only 'cos me dad were too tight to buy a new one.

She opens it and rummages around looking at the old discarded clothes inside. She pulls out a yellow fifties dress which is rather flamboyant. Mark sits on one of the dining-chairs and holds his head in his hands, waiting

Betty Look at that, I wondered where it had got to. This was my favourite. Look at the waist, just look at it, have you ever seen anything so little in your life? I don't know how I ever got into it. It had a little bolero, that just fitted round the top. I think I must have chucked that out. There must be three yards of material in this skirt, it used to swing right out when I spun round, those were the days. Conway Twitty, silk stockings and thin thighs ... (*She sighs deeply for the days gone by*)

Mark lifts his head up

It's a long time since I danced.
Mark Try it on.
Betty (*laughing*) You daft h'a'porth, it won't fit me now.
Mark Well just try it and see. Go on. We've still got time.
Betty I haven't got the underskirts.
Mark It doesn't matter. I'll tell you what, I'll look for them while you put the dress on.
Betty Are you sure?
Mark Yeh, go on. Get cracking, eh?

She starts to put the dress on as Mark rummages in the case

Betty It won't fit ... (*She is about to put the dress over her shoulders, then shouts*) Mark!
Mark What?
Betty I won't know how many bottles of milk to have delivered.

Beat

Mark Try the dress on ... (*Looking in another case*) Do you think they'll be in here?
Betty They might be, or in that trunk, have a look in there.

Mark goes over to the trunk and rummages around while Betty takes her overall off and tries to put the dress on over the top of her suit. He finds some net underskirts

I used to wear this to go to the Mecca Locarno, it was the big bands and Jimmy Savile in those days. I've talked to him you know.
Mark Yeh. You told me.
Betty Ohhhh! It smells of bath cubes. Lily of the Valley or is it ... (*she gets the dress stuck over her head*) Mark! Mark! I'm stuck. You'll have to help me, love.

Mark tries to help his mother pull the dress down over her head, but it won't shift

Mark It's all right, don't panic, I've got it.
Betty If I can just get me arm through ...
Mark Can you manage?
Betty (*struggling*) No, I don't think it's going to go. I think it's stuck.
Mark Pull your shoulders in.
Betty It's not me shoulders that's the problem.
Mark It's all right.

He manages to pull the dress over her head. It rips slightly

There!

Betty's head comes through the top of the dress, her hair dishevelled

Betty What do you think?
Mark Hang on a minute.
Betty It's a bit tight.
Mark Brilliant. It looks fantastic.
Betty (*turning her back towards Mark*) Zip it up?

It's obvious the dress won't zip, but Mark struggles away, trying to force the zip up. He manages to fasten the hook and eye at the top

Mark (*white lie*) It's just half an inch off.
Betty I'll breath in.
Mark It might just need letting out a bit.
Betty (*picking up a sash from the suitcase*) Never mind, pass me the underskirts.

Mark glances at his watch before he picks up the net underskirts. He looks at her

Turn around.

Mark turns his back on his mother as she pulls the underskirts up under her dress — even though the dress doesn't fit, she looks younger. The vibrant colour of the material suits her complexion and the tussled look to her hair is more flattering than the set curls

Of course they need starching, they're a bit flat. There!

Mark (*turning around*) You look great.
Betty Really?
Mark Really. Dead groovy.

Betty does a twirl revealing at least a six-inch gap where the zip doesn't meet

Why don't we go down and show Dad.
Betty (*going over to the box of old records and searching through*) I've not put it on for your father ... (*She pulls out a record*) Oh! Look, it's the Platters. Do you know this was the first record I bought ... (*She puts the record on*) ... or was it Paul Anka's "Diana", I can't remember, it was one or the other ...

Music plays: The Platters, "Twilight Time"

(*Listening*) Just listen to that. It's like drinking a carton of double cream.

She dances round the attic singing to the song. Mark rubs his head and looks at his watch. Betty grabs his hand

Come on dance with your mam. Oh! Come on.
Mark If you'll come down after we've finished?
Betty All right. Just listen to the music and let yourself go ...

They dance

That's it. It's easy as pie ...

They dance together. Betty sings. We hear banging on the flap. The record jumps. Betty goes over to the gramophone and takes the record off

Donald (*off*) Betty!
Mark We're up here, Dad!
Donald (*off*) Is your mother with you?!
Mark Yeh!
Betty Traitor!
Donald (*off*) What's she doing up there?
Mark We'll be down in a minute.
Donald (*off*) Your Margaret's here! I'm putting the kettle on.

They wait. Nothing happens

Mark Let's go and have a cup of tea with Aunty Margaret.

Betty I don't want a cup of tea.

Mark You said if I danced with you, you'd come down.

Betty I lied.

Mark Right, that's it! I've had enough. If you don't want to come to my wedding, then that's your choice. You know what this is, don't you? It's emotional blackmail. You're emotionally blackmailing your own son. Well it's not on. I'm not having it. You're supposed to be me mother, you're supposed to act in a motherly way, this is not a motherly way, Mother, do you understand?

Betty Yes.

Mark I've been up here nearly half an hour, trying to reason with you, but you won't listen, so I might as well go down. I'm getting married whether you're there or not. I'd like you to be there, I'd love you to be there, in fact I'll be very upset if you're not there, but if that's what you want then it's up to you. All right?! ... Now, I'm going down. (*He goes over to the gramophone and moves it*) I'm going down ... I mean it ... That is it. (*He lifts the flap up and throws it to one side*) I can't believe you're doing this to me. (*Levering himself down*) You've let me down, Mother.

He disappears down the flap

Betty (*small voice*) Mind your back.

Pause; Betty sways from side to side, almost childlike, her hands caressing the soft yellow material of the dress. Then she goes over to the flap and puts it back over the hole

I had him right here in this house, down there, in the front bedroom. Eighteen hours I was in labour, but the minute they put him in my arms I forgot all about the pain, he was the loveliest baby I'd ever seen, he made up for everything ... (*She reflects*) Sister Bower delivered him, she were a bossy sort, eighteen stone with a hairy mole on the end of her chin, she shouted at the poor student midwife, till she had her in such a dither she dropped the afterbirth, it went everywhere and Donald had just decorated, we tried sponging the wallpaper, but it brought the pattern off, it was cheap stuff. (*She reflects*) I had a proper confinement, fourteen days in bed, none of this forty-eight hour malarky they have nowadays, me mother stayed with us, she did all the washing and made sure Donald had his dinner, which was good of her, 'cos she never really took to him, she said he had close-set eyes, said she didn't like his accent, said he had a greedy streak ... she was right. (*She goes over to the records again and starts to look through them*) He wasn't like that in the beginning, if I'd asked for the moon he'd have reached up and got me it, he used to take me dancing, for a fish and chip supper, pictures every Saturday night, but the day we got married he changed, it was like he'd had a brain transplant, everything stopped, we didn't go out any more, he said he was saving up, he said he wanted a list of what I'd spent the housekeeping on ... that's when me back trouble started ... Oh! Johnny Mathis, I used to love Johnny Mathis ... (*She puts the record on*) Him and Frankie Vaughan.

She sways gently to the music, clutching the material of the dress, listening to the words. The song has a profound, memorable effect on her, reminds her of someone, another time. She spins round and the skirt of the dress swirls out in a cascade of colour. A glitter ball descends, the lighting changes and suddenly we are in a different mood and a different place — a dance hall of the late fifties, with glittering lights. She dances with great ease and confidence. She sweeps around the floor, singing along with the music. She passes by the alcove where the roof dips into a recess, looking totally radiant

She dances into the light again and she is dancing with Craze, a dark-haired, tall, muscular-built, imposing sort of man in his early thirties. He is dressed in late 1950s fashion. They sing together as though it were perfectly natural and they dance effortlessly around the floor

The loft flap opens with a bang and immediately the lights revert to their original state and the music stops. Mark's head appears

Mark All right, you win!

Betty and Craze stand motionless, still in the dance position, arms around one another, staring at Mark as he lifts himself into the loft

I'm not getting married. Not without you there I'm not.

He lifts one of the dining-room chairs off the stack, and sits on it

You've won. Are you happy now?

No answer. Betty is transfixed, still holding on to Craze. She slowly turns and looks at Craze and realizes he is still there. She screams

Betty Ahhhh! (*She lets go of Craze, runs over to the gramophone player and hides behind it*)
Mark Mam? ... What is it?

Betty Tell him to go away.
Mark Who?
Betty I don't want him to see me.
Mark Who are you on about?
Betty (*waving her arms about, not daring to look*) Him.
Mark Do you want me Aunty Margaret to call the doctor?
Betty (*peeping over the top of the record-player with her hands over her face*) He's looking at me.
Mark There's nobody there.
Betty There is.
Mark Where? There's just me and you, that's all.
Betty (*to the man*) Stop looking at me.
Mark It's all right, Mum. There's nobody looking at you.
Betty I don't want him to see me.
Mark Shall I call the doctor?
Betty No. Can't you see him?

Mark goes to where his mother is pointing. He swings his arms around, narrowly missing Craze. Craze ducks

Mark I'm telling you, Mam. There's nobody here ...

He swings the other way. Craze ducks again

You're just imagining it.
Betty I'm not.
Mark Look, you don't have to do this, Mam. If me marrying Jo upsets you that much, I've decided I'm not going through with it. So there you are ... (*Beat*) It's all off ... (*Beat*) If that's what you want ... (*Beat*) It's up to you ... (*Beat*) Do you hear what I'm saying? ... (*Beat*) Are you going to speak to me, Mother? ... (*Beat*) Will you answer me!!!
Craze I think he wants you to say something.
Betty (*shocked*) He talks.
Mark Mam!
Betty Go away!
Mark I'm trying to help you. I'm trying to make today easier for you.
Betty (*to Craze*) I don't know what to say.
Mark Thank you.
Craze He can't see me, or hear me.
Mark Come on, Mum.
Betty I thought you were dead.
Craze I am.
Mark Dead?
Craze Why didn't you write back?

Mark What are you talking about, dead? I'm not dead, I might be daft, but I'm definitely not dead.
Betty I'm not talking to you. I'm talking to him.

Mark moves over towards his mother, thinking she's talking to him

Mark It's all right, Mum, you don't have to keep on. You've won.
Craze I wanted you so much.
Betty I don't want you to look at me.
Mark I'm not. Just take the dress off.
Betty I've grown old.
Mark Aunty Margaret'll do your hair / and you'll look great.
Craze You're beautiful.
Betty You always had a smooth tongue.
Mark Pardon?
Craze All the better to kiss you with.
Betty Stop it! You're making me blush.
Mark Mam!
Craze My passionate Betty.
Betty Oh dear! I don't believe this.
Mark Don't you feel well?
Craze Kiss me all over you'd say to me.
Betty I never said that.
Mark Well, you look a bit odd.
Craze You were hungry and beautiful ——
Mark (*still waiting for his answer*) Mam?
Craze — and out of control and I loved you for it.
Betty That wasn't me. I was somebody else then.
Mark When? One of us is going mad.
Craze I can still smell your scent.
Betty God! I'm having a hot flush.
Mark (*thinking he's got his answer*) It's all right, Aunty Margaret was right, we'll ring the doctor.
Betty I don't need a bloody doctor! I just need ...
Mark What?
Betty To ... I don't know ... (*To Craze*) Say something else!
Mark It's all been too much for you. It'll be all right. I'm sorry. You just sit there and ...
Betty Mark! I'm telling you, there's someone here.
Mark Yes, Mum. Little green men with yellow wellies.
Betty Someone I knew a long time ago, before you were born.
Mark (*deciding to humour her*) Oh really. How interesting. Whereabouts exactly, Mother? Over here?
Betty No.

Mark Here?

Betty No.

Mark Swinging from the light bulb?

Betty No!! (*Pointing*) He's there. I can't believe you can't see him. He's just there.

Mark moves over to where Betty is pointing. Craze moves to where Betty is still hiding

Betty (*to Craze*) No! Stay still.

Mark thinks she's talking to him and he stays still

Not you, him!

Mark This is getting silly.

Betty (*moving to the other side of the gramophone*) He's moved. He's stood over there now.

Mark Well, I'll take your word for it.

Betty His name's Craze.

Mark Short for Crazy.

Betty Short for Alexander Krazenovski. His parents were Polish. He used to live in the flat below me and your dad at Reginald Terrace.

Craze ⎱ (*together*) ⎰ Number three.
Mark ⎰   ⎱ Right. And he's here, is he?

Betty Stood right there.

Mark And is this where you usually meet or is it ——

Betty No, I've not seen him since we moved.

Craze And anyway, I'm dead.

Betty And anyway, he's dead.

Mark Oh! I see. So he's a ghost, is he?

Craze I don't like "ghost".

Betty He doesn't like you calling him "ghost"

Mark No, I'm not too keen meself.

Craze Just like you don't like "Mother".

Betty You've been listening.

Mark Well, I'm sorry. My apologies.

Craze Accepted.

Betty Accepted.

Mark So you thought you'd see him today, did you? Sort of catch up with everything.

Betty No, he just came. I didn't plan it.

Craze Liar!

Betty I didn't!

Mark I believe you.

Betty He just appeared from nowhere.

Craze I think you're going to have a problem with this.

Mark So what you're saying is he's somebody you used to know that lived at Reginald Terrace, only he's dead?

Craze He's a bright boy.

Betty I mean he's not got a white sheet over his head and making funny noises, but he's definitely dead.

Short pause, while Mark thinks what to do next

Mark Does he want to come to the wedding?

Betty I don't know, I could ask him.

Mark 'Cos he won't need a car, will he? I mean he could just transport himself to the church, he could be the holy spirit if he likes, and then he could just hover about at the reception, I don't think anybody'd mind.

Craze He doesn't believe you.

Betty I'm telling you, Mark. He's right here.

Mark Well perhaps he would do some ghostly things like ... moving that paint pot off that chair and making it fly across the room.

Craze I don't do funny tricks.

Betty He doesn't do funny tricks. He won't believe me unless you do.

Craze Is it important that he does?

Mark Mum! Please ...

Betty What?

Craze He thinks you've flipped.

Betty I wish I hadn't told you now. Go get married. I don't want you up here. I don't want to talk to you anymore. I want to be left alone.

Mark With the ghost.

Craze You had your first feeling with me.

Betty Stop it! I wish you wouldn't talk like that.

Mark Like what?

Betty Not you. It's very embarrassing in front of my son.

Mark What's he doing?

Craze He can't hear.

Mark I said, what's he doing?

Betty Nothing. We had a bit of a thing once, that's all.

Mark ⎫
Craze ⎭ (*together*) A thing?

Betty Well, what else do you want me to call it?

Mark What sort of a thing?

Craze A love affair. Do you still have that birthmark on your bottom?

Betty (*excruciatingly embarrassing for her; to Craze*) Please.

Mark (*thinking he has to say please for the information*) Please.
Craze Shaped like a little strawberry.
Betty It's more like a map of South America these days.
Mark What's South America got to do with it?
Betty Look, I'm getting very confused. I can't speak to you both at the same time.

Betty goes over to the gramophone and pulls a record out of its cover. She puts her hand in between the cover as:

Mark You're confused! You want to try it from where I am.

Betty pulls out an old letter and hands it to Mark

Betty Read this.
Mark What is it?
Craze (*approaching Betty*) I've never been able to eat a strawberry without thinking of you and that little pink mark ——

Craze goes right up to Betty; Betty backs into the gramophone

Betty (*to Craze*) What are you doing?
Mark I'm reading it.

Craze pulls Betty to him, she gasps. Mark continues to read the letter. They are standing together, but Craze and Betty ignore Mark. He puts his hand on her bottom, over the top of her skirt

Craze — it was about here ... (*running his hand down her leg*) ... and those beautiful long legs that used to wrap around me ... (*moving his hand back up her leg and towards ...*) and those soft, wet, velvet folds waiting for me to ...
Mark Mam?
Betty Oh! Shut up, you've got the rest of your life; all I've got is now.
Mark Who wrote this?
Betty Him.
Craze Let me see. (*He snatches the letter off Mark*)

Mark screams out in astonishment as he sees the letter floating through the air

Mark Ahh!! Who's doing that?
Craze You kept it.

Mark It's some kind of trick, isn't it?

Betty goes over and tries to get the letter out of Craze's hand. Craze holds the letter up high and walks about reading the letter. Betty follows him around

Betty The only letter you ever wrote to me.

Craze "My darling Betty. When am I going to see you again? / My life seems so empty without ..."

Mark (*unnerved, starting to breath heavily*) All right. I give in. How are you doing it?

Betty I told you.

Craze I was quite a poet.

Betty You were all talk.

Craze Was I?

Mark I am going mad ... (*deep breath*) my mother's talking to a ghost ... (*deep breath*) my father's going berserk downstairs ... (*deep breath*) there's letters flying about the loft ... (*deep breath*) and I'm getting married in less than an hour ... (*He continues to breathe heavily*)

Craze I think he's hyperventilating. Have you got a bag?

Betty A bag? Oh! A bag! Just a minute! Don't faint ... (*She races over and grabs a brown carrier bag full of Christmas cards*) Keep breathing ... (*She tips the Christmas cards on the floor*) Get your head in there ...

Mark breaths deeply into the bag as he tries to get control. Betty instructs him

(*Instructing him*) In ... out ... that's it. And in ... and out ... nice and steady ... in and out ...

Betty looks at Craze and she sits next to Mark. Mark continues to breathe heavily throughout the following

Betty I've got fat, haven't I?

Craze You were never thin.

Betty I was. I had a twenty-four inch waist once ... You just look the same.

Craze That's the best thing about dying.

Betty I had to read it in the newspaper.

Craze Were you upset?

Betty I came up here and read your letter.

Craze And that was the first time you talked to me.

Mark takes his face away from the bag

Betty Did you hear?

Craze (*noticing Mark*) I think he's getting better.

Mark (*still breathless*) Who was he?

Betty Just someone who lived beneath us.

Craze laughs at her choice of words

He had a very common wife, she had a foul mouth, bleached her hair and told him it was natural ...

Craze She was a natural ...

Betty Mousey, that's what she was, mousey and trying to make up for it. She used to wander round with next to no clothes on. She did!

Mark Why didn't you ever tell me about him?

Betty I didn't like to.

Mark Why not? We talked about everything else. You could have told me. I thought we could talk about anything.

Betty We could.

Craze You used to tell me everything once upon a time.

Betty When you were alive ... (*to Mark*) I'm sorry I'm / talking ——

Mark Talking to him ... / it's all right, I can handle this.

Craze And when I was first dead, you used to come up here and tell me things, like where you'd been and what you'd done, you'd tell me about Margaret and ...

Betty And then I stopped.

Mark What?

Betty Talking to him, I suppose because I started to tell you.

Mark No, you definitely never told me about him; in fact, you've never mentioned him.

Betty Because I didn't want you to feel bad about me.

Craze Thanks.

Betty (*to Craze*) Well, it's not a very nice thing for your son to ...

Mark (*thinking she's talking to him*) I'd have understood, or at least I think I would. What about me dad?

Betty He never knew.

Mark Why did you stay with him?

Craze The million dollar question!

Betty Would you have left Moira?

Mark Moira? Who's Moira?

Betty (*to Mark, of Craze*) I'm talking to him. I'm sorry love, but he keeps / interrupting.

Craze It was you that moved away.

Betty I had to. It wasn't up to me. Donald put a deposit down on this house.

I was pregnant, I couldn't stay in that pokey little flat. Not with a baby on the way ...

Mark Hang on a minute, pregnant?!

Betty With you.

Mark With me?

Betty I've only been pregnant once, Mark.

Mark Er ... can I, er, just get something straight?

Betty Yes?

Mark Well, it's a bit awkward is this, but ... is me dad, me dad?

Beat. Both men wait for the answer

Craze Well, answer him. Tell him yes.

Betty Why?

Mark Because I'd like to know, that's why. I mean, if all this happened thirty-two years ago, anything could be ... well, he might be me dad.

Betty That's right.

Mark So?

Betty So, does it matter?

Mark Course it bloody matters.

Betty Don't swear.

Mark It's my wedding day, for Christ's sake.

Donald (*off*) Mark! Is she coming down?

Mark (*hushed*) I'd like to know who my real father is if you don't mind. I mean if it's not too much to ask.

Donald Mark!

Mark (*calling*) Yeh! She's coming down.

Donald (*off*) I don't know what you think you're playing at, Betty.

Betty Strip poker!

Donald (*off*) I'm coming up.

Betty If he comes up here, that's it. I'm never coming down.

Mark No. It's all right, Dad! I've got it all under control.

Donald (*off*) It's bloody ridiculous, is this! Margaret wants to know if she should ring the doctor.

Betty She can ring Pope John Paul for all I care.

Mark I want you at my wedding.

Betty Go see to your dad. I just need to be on my own for a bit.

Mark I don't think I should leave you.

Betty I'm not going anywhere, am I?

Mark Five minutes, then.

Betty That'll be fine.

Mark 'Cos we'll have to be setting off soon. Bridegroom's got to be there first.

Betty Don't worry.
Mark Right then ... (*Whispering*) Has he gone now?

Craze sits on a crate, watching them

Betty Yeh.
Mark I wouldn't say anything to me dad about it ... about him.
Betty That's right.
Mark You scared me a bit.
Betty I know.
Mark (*still trying to work it out*) That letter flying about.
Betty I'm sorry, love.
Mark I really thought ...

Betty stops him with her reassuring smile

There must have been a draught ...

Betty keeps smiling. Mark takes this to mean "yes"; he's relieved. He lifts the flap

You sure you don't want us to call the doctor?
Betty There's nothing wrong with me.
Mark I'll get your flower ready and the step-ladders.
Betty You do that.

Mark exits through the flap on to the landing

Craze So?
Betty So what happens now?
Craze It's up to you.
Betty Why are you here?
Craze Because you wanted me to be.
Betty You're not real, are you?
Craze I'm here.
Betty You're in my head ... I look ridiculous, don't I?
Craze The dress is a bit tight.
Betty Do you remember it?
Craze I bought it for you.
Betty That's right.
Craze Zip used to stick three inches from the bottom.

She stares at him

Betty Was I really passionate?

Craze Like a crazy woman. You were the most exciting thing that ever happened to me. I couldn't wait to see you. I used to hear you singing upstairs and I'd lie on the bed and imagine making love with you. I couldn't wait till the next time we could be together. Sometimes I used to lay awake on a night listening for the slightest sound coming from your bedroom. I used to think if I heard the bedsprings move once more, I'd go straight up there and kill him.

Betty (*laughing*) You were jealous ... (*She revels in the thought*) All that time, you were jealous, if only I'd've known ... (*She looks at him coyly*) Look how young you were.

Craze (*jesting*) Just a boy really.

Betty A handsome young man ... You used to buy me a Babycham.

Craze Or two. Sometimes, you'd have three.

Betty (*enjoying the moment as she reflects*) And we'd dance the night away.

Craze (*correcting her as he takes his jacket off and lays it on the floor*) Till ten ——

Betty (*interjecting*) Half-past!

Craze — and then you'd have to be back so that Donald didn't worry, but we'd stop in the park by the cricket pavilion.

Craze sits next to the jacket and pulls Betty down to the side of him like he used to do in the cricket pavilion. Lights change to reflect an evening in the park

Betty And then I'd be late and I'd have to run like mad.

Craze I'd wait till you turned the corner and then I'd set off.

Betty I used to listen for the front door closing so that I'd know you'd be in safe ...

Beat. They look at one another, reflecting on their time together

God, I loved you so much ... I thought when I left, when I stopped seeing you, that it would just go away, I'd stop thinking about you, I'd stop imagining what it would be like to be ... with you ... but it didn't stop, it didn't go away, it just grew stronger ... and then I found out you'd died. It was our Margaret's birthday and I was in the post office when who should walk in but Mr Solomon, you remember him, flat five. He said, "Hallo, Betty", I hardly recognized him, 'cos he was so grey, even his beard. Anyway, he's living in the Newbury's, I expect he's dead now ... He said, "How are you keeping, girl?" I said, "Very well, thank you." He asked after our Mark. I told him he'd started school and then he said it. I remember his precise words. He said, "Did you hear about him that lived on the bottom floor?" My heart nearly stopped. I said, "Who?" He said, "Flat three with the common wife" and I knew then that something awful had happened. I could feel it. I knew before he'd even said it. I said, "No. What?" He said he'd read it in the paper last week. "He was shot dead, love," he said, "a bullet straight through his back." I thought nobody's shot dead, not in real life, that sort of thing only happens in the pictures, I thought he must have got it wrong ... I didn't hear anymore ... I forgot me postal order ... (*Tears trickle down her face, she wipes them away*) I went home, searched the house for last week's *Evening News* and then I found it wrapped round the potato peelings in the bin and there you were smiling out at me, like you always smiled. Stop looking so smug with yourself ... (*She hits him*) What did you go and die for you stupid ... stupid, bloody thing ... (*continuing to hit him*) I hate you for that.

Craze holds her. She stops hitting him

Craze (*embracing her*) It's all right ... It's all right, my beautiful Betty! ... Don't cry.
Betty I'm not going down ... It's not that I don't want him to get married, 'cos I do, I want him to be happy, but how can I stand there and smile when I see the only good thing in my life slipping away. I know why you've come and I'm glad, 'cos that's what I want. There's nothing for me here now, so take me with you. Help me to go ... please.

The Lights go down on Betty and Craze as they kiss

ACT II

Twenty minutes later

Everything is as it was left at the end of Act I, except for the skylight, now slightly open (although it should by no means draw attention to itself). After a moment the loft lid is knocked off with some force. Two hands appear on the frame and Donald lifts himself into view. Donald is a wiry, aggressive, little man in his mid to late fifties. He is dressed in his wedding outfit — tails, cravat and buttonhole

Donald Betty! ... Your mother's rung! ... Betty!!! (*He looks about*) She's not here.

Mark (*off*) She must be there.

Donald (*levering himself into the loft*) I'm telling you she's definitely not here.

Mark's head takes the place of his father's in the loft opening; he also wears tails, cravat and buttonhole

Donald searches round the loft, looking for Betty

Mark Well, where is she?

Donald I don't know, if I knew I wouldn't be asking you, would I? You said she was coming down.

Mark That's what she told me.

Donald This is getting bloody ridiculous. Betty!

Mark levers himself into the loft

Mark Mam!

Donald Are you sure she was definitely up here?

Mark Course she was. You heard her, she spoke to you.

Donald Well, where's she gone?

Mark There is nowhere; she didn't come past us.

Donald (*looking for her*) So she must be still up here. Betty! Come on, "game's up". We've got to go. Stop playing silly buggers, your Margaret and her fancy man's here.

Mark Mam!

Donald We've got to be setting off in a minute. Betty!
Mark She's not here.
Donald Well, I can see that, can't I? What did you say to her?
Mark Nothing. I asked her to come down, that's all.
Donald You must have said something.
Mark Oh! That's right, blame me.
Donald Well you were the last one with her.
Mark I told her I wanted her to come to my wedding, that's all.
Donald Of course she's coming to your wedding, she's your mother. You've probably upset her now, started her off.
Mark I haven't "started her off". It's nothing to do with me.
Donald Meaning?
Mark (*not wanting to argue*) Nothing.
Donald No, come on, if you're going to say something, you might as well say it, let's have it out.
Mark Look, I'm not arguing with you, Dad, I haven't got time.
Donald No, you never have. Plenty of time for your mother, though.
Mark Dad. I'm getting married in half an hour, / I'll be setting off in less than ——
Donald Meaning *I've* set her off. That's what you mean, I know, I'm not stupid. Meaning she's up here 'cos I've upset her.
Mark I didn't say that.
Donald You don't need to, it's implied, you and your mother have this knack of saying one thing and communicating something else.
Mark Look, let's just keep calm and ——
Donald Calm! I'm perfectly calm, calm is my second name.
Mark Well, what are you shouting for then?
Donald Because I don't know where your mother is, that's why.
Mark We'll find her, she can't be far.
Donald You're right, you're absolutely one hundred per cent correct, she can only be inside the house or outside the house, there is nowhere else for her to go, is there?
Mark That's right.

Donald makes his way back over to the loft entrance, preparing to go back down

Donald I've had a terrible week with her, you know, in fact I've had a terrible month, everything I say is wrong, she snaps my head off for the slightest thing — you don't see it. I know she's at a funny age, but she's no need to be like that. I'm not saying anything behind her back that I wouldn't say to her face, I've told her they can give her things to make it easier, hormone tablets. I've seen it on the telly, I've told her to get to the doctors.

Mark Well, maybe you should talk to her, instead of telling her.

Donald stands again

Donald She doesn't want to talk to me, you're the only one she wants to talk to.

Mark You don't try, Dad.

Donald Try! I've tried till I'm blue in the face, she doesn't listen to me, anyway you shouldn't have to try when you've been married to someone for over thirty years.

Mark No, you've got it wrong, you've got to try even harder. / You've got to ——

Donald Listen, when you've been married to Jo as long as I've been married to your mother then you can stand there and argue the toss with me.

Mark I'm not arguing with you, all I'm / saying is ——

Donald I'll tell you something and I've never said this to another living soul ... (*lowering his voice*) but your mother's a very difficult woman to live with.

Mark I've lived with her and / I don't think she's difficult.

Donald You've not *lived* with her, you've been *adored* by her, you've been put on a pedestal by her, she worships the toilet seat that you sit on, it's Mark this, Mark that, this is for our Mark, that's for our Mark, do you think our Mark'd like this. Do you think our Mark'd like that. She's doted on you and that's different.

Mark Because she's got nobody else to dote on / that's why she ——

Donald What about me? / I'm her husband!

Mark I've watched how you are with her.

Donald Have you? Have you really? Go on then, what have you seen?

Mark I don't want to get into all that.

Donald No, come on, I want to know.

Mark Let's just find her shall we? It's quarter to ——

Donald I want to know what you think you've seen.

Mark All right! You don't appreciate her, that's what all *this* is about.

Donald All what?

Mark All this, Why do you think she came up here in the first place?

Donald That's easy. 'Cos she doesn't want you to get married, that's why. 'Cos she's got a very selfish streak has your mother.

Mark Well, I've never seen it.

Donald That's because it's all been directed at me, till now. I'll tell you something, and your Aunty Margaret'll agree with me here, your mam has been too much of a mother and not enough of a wife and that's the truth. She doesn't care about me, I can go to hell as long as you're all right. Well, how do you think that makes me feel? I don't like talking to you like this, but she won't let me near her ... it's three years since ... well, I'm only human. Think about it! Three years, well how would you like it? I know she wants single beds, I'm not stupid, she leaves the catalogue out at the appropriate page, she pretends it's 'cos of her back, she says we can push them together but I'm not having it, we've got to have some married life ... she won't even sit with me. I mean, that's not much to ask is it? I'll tell you something, there's been times, Mark, when I have seriously considered leaving your mother but because I care about her and because I believe that marriage and fatherhood is a commitment / I've stuck with it.

Mark Oh! For Christ's sake, shut up!

Donald Hey! Who do you think you're talking to?

Mark You sound like a right pompous arse.

Donald You cheeky bastard!

Mark I don't know why she ever stayed with you.

Donald You're not too big you know.

Mark For what?

Donald You know for what.

Mark No, come on, tell me, I want to hear it.

Donald You think you know everything, don't you. You think you know it all.

Mark Well, I know a damn sight more than you do.

Donald (*taking his jacket off*) Oh! Do you really? Well, we'll see about that.

Mark Why, what yer going to do? Hit me? ... (*He takes his jacket off*) Go on, then, right there. Go on.

They circle like boxers in a ring. It looks like Donald might, but then he bottles out

Donald You'll not get up again if I do.

Mark Well, I'm shaking in me boots ... (*he continues circling*)

Donald (*backing off now*) I've done the best I can for you and your mother.

Mark (*sarcastically*) Yeh course / you have.

Donald I kept a roof over your head and food on the table.

Mark (*sarcastically*) What more could we want?

Donald Yes, well you want to try it.

Mark And what about affection, eh?

Donald moves DS

(*Following him*) Did you ever show us any of that? Come on think, try and remember!

Donald (*moving away*) You don't know you're born / you.

Mark (*following*) Did you ever put your arm round me and give me a hug? No, I don't think so! Did you ever sit me on your knee and read me a story? No! Can't quite remember that! Did you ever tuck me up in bed and tell me you loved me? No! Not that I can recollect! Did you ever ruffle my hair and tell me well done, son? No. Never, not once.

Donald Because you got all that from your mother, she spoilt you rotten.

Mark Maybe she was just trying to make up for what you couldn't give me.

Donald When you were little, I used to tell you stories and play football with you and take you fishing but you won't remember that.

Mark I bet you never tell her that you love her either.

Donald I'm going down.

Mark I don't think I've ever seen you put so much as an arm round her.

Donald You can think what you want.

Mark Or just smile at her, or look at her in a loving way. I don't think I've ever heard you even say thank you.

Donald I've said plenty of "thank yous" in my time.

Mark Not that I've heard.

Donald Well, maybe you weren't in earshot ——

Mark laughs scathingly

—— and there's more ways of saying thank you than stringing a couple of words together, you know.

Mark You used to come home from work, take your boots off, go through into room and wait for me mam to bring your dinner through ...

Donald Rubbish! / You've got it all ——

Mark You did! I remember once watching her make you the whole works, roast beef, Yorkshire pudding, two veg and potatoes, she fussed round warming your plate, making sure your potatoes had no lumps and your meat wasn't too fatty. She put salt and pepper on the tray and took it through to you. I thought, "Go on, say it, just say the magic word", like you said I should always say, but you never took your eyes off that screen, and when you finally did look down at your dinner, do you know what you said?

Donald I'm sure you're going to tell me.

Mark Gravy!

Donald No, I didn't ——

Mark Gravy! That's what you said! / Yes, Dad, you did, I saw it with my own eyes, heard it with my own ears.

Donald And did you ever think to ask yourself why I was having me dinner on a tray? I'll tell you why, because you and her had already eaten that's why. She wouldn't wait till I came home, so that we could all sit down together and have a family meal. She said you were hungry when you came home from school, so you two'd have yours at half-past four and I'd have to sit by meself with only the six o'clock news for company. You never let me in, either of you, sometimes I felt like I was intruding in my own home ... anyway, this isn't the time or the place to start bringing all this up ...

Mark No, this is exactly the time and precisely the place to say what you think, 'cos it's now or never, I'll be gone tomorrow, so you might as well say it. Do you know she has an imaginary lover called Crazy? She talks to him, like he exists, that's what she was doing up here and I find that profoundly sad. That really hurts me, that my mother needs to do that, to create a world that is more blissful to her than this one. I think there is something deeply wrong that my mother has to do that and that worries me.

Donald She was *talking* to him?

Mark To herself.

Donald Up here.

Mark That's right. I'm stood here talking to her and she carries on talking to him ... it ... whatever. She says he's a ghost and I can't see him, she's got it all worked out; honest to God she had me believing it. She's even written herself a letter as though it's from him. It's here somewhere ... (*He looks for the letter*) This is it. Here, read it. (*He hands the letter to his father*) She said he used to live at ——

Donald She didn't write this.

Mark Well who did?

Donald He did.

Mark What are you saying?

Donald I'm saying she did have a bit of a fling, a long time ago, when we were first married but it was nothing. I never said anything. She got pregnant with you and we moved house. I made sure it was a long way away. It'd have taken her two buses to get to see him and two buses back. I thought things would get better and they did for a bit, well, for quite a while really ... I've known for a long time your mother didn't ... well, something was missing but ...

Mark (*softly, sensitive to his father's feelings*) But what?

Donald I knew she'd never leave me ... because ... well because I'm your father.

Mark (*stunned by the very thought of it*) You mean she stayed with you because of me?

Donald (*low*) Yes.

Mark And you knew that? ... My God! I don't believe it.

Donald I don't know what happened. She sort of went off me. That's what marriage is like, Mark. It's not all sex, Ovaltine and roses, you know. Sometimes it's hanging in there when you know you're not wanted.

Mark And now he's gone.

Donald That's right.

Mark And you'll be glad when I've gone, won't you?

Donald No. I'm happy that you've found someone you want to spend your life with.

Mark Tell the truth, Dad!

Donald No ... Well, I suppose a bit of me is, yes ... There was always sides, you see, and you were always on hers and I was always by meself, it gets to be a bit lonely sometimes. I just want your mother to want me ... (*Moved*) I'm going down. (*He tries to cover his emotions as he goes towards the loft opening to make his way back down*) She might have slipped out the back and gone to Mrs Cooper's or gone to the end to get some more confetti.

Mark Dad!

Donald What?

Mark goes to his dad and tries to hug him. Donald stands rigid

Donald What you doing, you daft thing.

Mark I'm holding you.

Donald stands stiffly, not knowing what to do with his arms. Then slowly he puts his arms round his son. The embrace ends. Donald searches for his handkerchief. He can't make eye contact with his son

Donald I think I'm ... coming down with a cold.

Mark I'm sorry.

Donald So am I. (*He blows his nose without looking at Mark. Embarrassed*) It's probably just the dust getting to me sinuses. Right well, I'll go to the newsagent if you check out Mrs Cooper's. (*He starts to lower himself down the loft entrance*)

Mark Dad!

Donald is half-way down the opening. He stops. He turns to look at his son. He meets his eyes. Beat

Donald Eh?

Mark Skylight's open.

Donald and Mark both look up to the slightly ajar skylight

Donald Eh?

Mark She wouldn't have gone up there, would she?

They both look over towards the open skylight

Donald No! What for?

Mark walks over to underneath the skylight and feels the water tank

Mark Well, it's definitely open.
Donald It must have been open before.
Mark It rained last night, tank's not wet.
Donald She can't have ——
Margaret (*off*) Donald!
Mark (*softly*) Tell her we'll be down in a minute.
Donald (*calling*) We'll be down in a minute, Margaret.
Margaret (*off*) Is she all right?
Donald She's fine, make yourself another cup of tea, make one for Mal.
Margaret (*off*) Shouldn't we be setting off?

Mark stands on the dining-room chair under the skylight

Mark It's only at the end of the street.
Margaret (*off*) Bridegroom should be there first.
Donald Yes, well he will be ...

Mark pushes the skylight open

Mark Mam!

The stage half rotates, so that we see a side, sliced section of the house and the roof

Betty is sitting on the roof clinging on to the chimney

Mark is standing on the dining-room chair — his head through the skylight, looking for his mother. Donald is still half through the loft entrance, his head and shoulders in the loft area

Donald Is she there?
Mark Mam!
Betty Yes?
Mark Oh! God.
Donald Mark?

Mark What are you doing, Mam?

Betty Admiring the view. They've been rushing in and out with the flowers.

Donald scrambles into the loft area

Donald Betty! Let me get up there.

Mark (*quietly*) Dad, just keep calm.

Donald Calm! I can't keep calm, me wife's on the roof and he's asking me to keep calm.

Betty You've got a lovely day for it ... Mrs Cooper's got all her washing out.

Donald Will you let me get up there?

Mark Dad! ... (*Calmly*) They've forecast gales for later on.

Betty Oh! No, I think it'll stay nice.

Mark How did you get over there?

Betty It was easy, I just walked, well sort of crawled really. Do you know I never realized number forty-seven had an extension on the back.

Donald What's she doing up there? / She's doing this on purpose. She's deliberately trying to ——

Betty Tell him to shut up.

Mark (*interjecting*) Have you got a rope? ... Dad! Listen to me. Is there a rope anywhere?

Donald I don't know.

Mark Well, look for one, or anything we can tie together.

Donald What are you going to do?

Mark I don't know yet, just find me one.

Donald I'm not looking for no rope, I'm ringing the police.

Betty If he rings the police, that's it.

Mark He's not ringing the police, he's definitely not ringing the police, no police right? ... Right?

Donald Right.

Betty Right ... You're going to be late for your wedding, love.

Mark Mum!

Betty Mark!

Mark What can I do?

Betty Nothing, love, I'm all right, honestly. I feel fine. I feel like I'm on me holidays. It's lovely. I haven't felt like this in ages.

Donald (*panicked, loudly*) I can't find a rope!

Betty He never looks properly. He's hopeless. He never moves anything. Tell him to look in the box next to the Christmas trimmings, there should be the old washing-line in there.

Mark Look in the box / next to ——

Donald I heard!

Mark Can I come and sit with you?

Betty No! It's dangerous, you could kill yourself if you fell.

Mark So could you, Mam.

Betty Ooooh! There's a car arriving ... (*stretching to see*) I think it's our Graham / and Elaine.

Mark Keep still! Will you stop moving about.

Betty It is, they're a bit early. I thought they'd have come to the house first.

Mark Just keep hold of the chimney, Mother.

Betty I bet it's 'cos our Margaret's here. Elaine and her have fallen out, because she won't let little James call her nanna.

Donald I've found it! ... Here, I've got it.

Mark Tie it round your middle.

Donald What?

Mark Just do as I say.

Donald ties the rope round his middle as Mark ties the other end of the rope round his waist

I'm coming over to sit with you, Mam, it's all right 'cos I'm going to tie a rope round me.

Betty Don't you dare.

Mark (*securing the rope and climbing out of the skylight*) And then I'm going to tie the rope around you and you're going to go back along the roof to me dad then you're going to throw the rope back for me and then I'm going to back along the roof and then we're all going to go down and then we're going to the church, all of us, together, because I need you there with me, do you understand?

Betty I'm perfectly all right here.

Donald What am I supposed to do now?

Mark Grab hold of something solid and don't let go.

Donald grabs hold of one of the beams as Mark tries to clamber on all fours on to the roof

Betty Be careful. You'll get yourself all filthy.

Mark clutches hold of the skylight frame. Betty clutches hold of the chimney as the stage rotates fully. We see the roof in all its glory — chimney, TV aerial, loose guttering, the odd broken slate. The inside of the loft is now out of view

Mark! What are you doing?

Mark I'm coming over.

Betty You won't be told, will you.

Mark (*to Donald*) Are you all right, Dad?

Donald (*off*) Fine! Are you sure you know what you're doing?

Mark You just keep hold of something solid.

Betty I'm not coming down, Mark.

Mark (*starting to crawl along the roof*) Well, you can't stop up here for ever, you'll have to come down sometime, so you might as well come down now.

Betty This is silly, for heaven's sakes.

Mark We'll go down together and we'll go to the church together and you can stand next to me and then we'll ring the travel agent and see if we can get an extra ticket for ——

Betty Stop it!

Mark What?

Betty I can't do that, you're getting married. I can't come with you. I've got to let go ...

With that Mark hits a loose slate and his leather-soled shoes fail to hold him. He slides down the roof on all fours. Betty and Mark scream together

Mark ⎫ (*together*) ⎧ Ahhhh!!!!
Betty ⎭   ⎨ Mark!!!!

Mark Dad!!!!

Betty Donald!!!!

The rope is pulled taut. Mark is precariously balanced, his foot lodged on the gutter but the majority of his body weight taken by the rope. He tries to grab the gutter

Betty Are you all right?

Mark Never better.

Betty I told you to get some rubber soles put on them shoes.

Mark Mam, it's hardly the time / to start ——

Betty Leather soles don't last two minutes, you could have killed yourself. Donald!!

No answer

Mark Dad!

No answer

Betty ⎫ (*together; bellowing*) ⎰ Donald!!!!
Mark ⎭   ⎱ Dad!!!!

Craze pops his head through the skylight

Craze He's not there!
Betty Well, where is he?
Mark Holding the other end. Dad?
Craze He isn't.
Mark Can you hear me, Dad?! Why isn't he answering?
Betty He's gone.
Mark Gone! What do you mean, he's gone? He's at the other end.
Craze It's tied to the beam.

Betty stands up

Betty It's tied to the beam, it's all right though 'cos I can crawl back over there / and get you ...
Mark No, Mam!!! You just stay where you are.
Betty If I got over here, I can get back again.
Mark Just stay there. Dad! Dad!!
Betty I've told you, he's not there.
Mark How do you know?
Betty 'Cos Craze told me.
Mark Not him again! Not now. Dad!! Where the bloody hell is he?
Betty Language, Mark!
Mark I'm going to fall.
Betty No, you're not, I'm coming / over to ——
Mark Will you stay where you are!
Betty I can do it.
Mark No, Mam! Please stay where you are.
Betty Craze said I can, he'll look after me, won't you?
Mark You'll fall.

Craze holds out his hand to Betty

Craze It's easy.
Mark Don't! Just wait for me dad.
Betty I can't, Mark.
Mark Of course you can.
Betty You'll be all right, love.
Mark No, I won't. Stay there.

Craze My beautiful Betty! Come to me.

There is a moment: Betty, trance-like, is about to leave the chimney pot and walk to Craze. Then we hear Donald's voice

Donald (*off*) Betty!
Mark Dad! Where've you been?

Donald's head and shoulders appear from over the back diagonal slope of the roof

We might just see the top of a ladder. Betty stands still. Craze remains at the skylight

Donald What's going on?
Mark Stop her, Dad.
Donald What do you think you're playing at, Betty?

Donald pulls Betty out of her trance-like state

Craze What ever did you see in him?
Betty I don't know.
Donald You can't carry on like this. Your mother's waiting for us to pick her up.
Betty He was a very good dancer once.
Donald Who was?
Mark I thought you were in the loft.
Donald I went to borrow Mr Cooper's ladders ... (*He sees Mark*) What you doing there?
Mark Oh! You know, hanging about, sunbathing, what do you think?
Betty You do say the silliest things sometimes, Donald.
Donald That gutter's not safe. It's old. It's ready to give.
Mark Well, you were supposed to be on the other end of the rope, that's what we decided.
Donald That's what *you* decided. *I* decided to borrow Mr Cooper's ladders.
Betty He always has to have his own way.
Donald Own way! It's not a question of having my own way, it's a question of what's best. I think I know what's best for my own wife.
Betty Well that's where you're wrong, Donald, because you've never known what's best for *me*.
Donald Well what do you want me to do, let you fall off the roof?
Betty If that's what I want, yes.

Donald And what about me and Mark, don't we count?

Betty Not right now, no.

Donald Well that's a lovely attitude to take, and you accuse me of wanting my own way!

Betty I don't want you up here, either of you. I came up here to be on my own. I wish you'd both just go away. / I just want to be left alone.

Mark (*trying to get a word in edgeways*) Ermm ... can I just ... / Will somebody ...

Donald (*ignoring Mark*) Well you picked the right day for it, didn't you?

Betty I didn't pick anything, I just went into the loft to tidy round, that's all, sort things out, make sure our Mark hadn't left anything and if you'd have left me alone I'd have come back down, / but no, you have to follow me around all the time asking what I'm doing, who I'm talking to and what about. I can't have a minute to meself.

Mark (*trying to get a word in edgeways*) I don't like interrupting, but ——

Donald You see what she's like, that's what I get if I talk to her, that's why I watch the television. / I can't do right for doing wrong.

Mark Look! Do you think ——

Betty (*to Donald*) You don't talk to me, you natter me. We don't have conversations, you tell me what I should and shouldn't be doing, that isn't talking to someone. You don't know the meaning of the word.

Donald Are you listening to this. I hope your wife doesn't talk to you like that.

Mark I hate to mention / this but I'm hanging here by a ——

Betty She won't because she won't need to, she might have a nose in the air sometimes but she knows a good husband when she sees one.

Donald And I suppose I'm a bad husband, am I?

Betty Yes.

Donald Then why did you stay with me?

Betty I don't know! Because I was barmy, that's why ...

Donald Well, you should have gone with him, 'cos I'd have been better off without you.

Betty Well, I'm going off with him now.

Donald You what?

Craze That's right, you tell him.

Betty And you can shut up!

Donald I haven't said anything.

Betty I'm leaving you. I don't blame you entirely for being a bad husband, 'cos I let you be like that. I've been doing a lot of thinking these last couple of weeks and especially these past couple of hours and I've come to the conclusion that it's not all your fault; if I'd have been different then maybe you would have been but it's too late now, we're too old to change so ——

There is a loud crack. Mark jerks suddenly as the gutter starts to give. Mark grabs tight hold of the rope. There are gasps from down below

Mark Ahhhh! Will somebody help me please!!!?
Betty Help him, will you.
Donald I told you it wouldn't last.
Craze And the rope's starting to give.
Betty The rope's started to give.
Mark Help!
Donald How do you know?
Betty Because ... because I know it is. Move your ladder round the front.
Donald I can't because the porch is in the way.
Mark Do something / will you?
Betty Well, put the ladder on the porch roof.
Donald I can't, it slopes.
Betty Oh! Yes, I forgot. What are we going to do?
Donald I don't know, you just stay there.
Mark I'm not going anywhere.

Donald goes back down the ladder

Mark Don't be long.
Donald (*off*) Nobody panic. I've got this under control.
Betty It's all right, love.
Mark Don't mind me, I'm having a wonderful time.
Betty I see we've got an audience.
Mark Morning, Mrs Cooper! Enjoying the show, are you?

We hear chatter from down below

Betty I thought she'd be out gawping, her and that scraggy-haired daughter.

The gutter cracks again. Mark grabs hold of the rope. Gasps from the crowd

Mark } (*together*) { Shit!!
Betty }   { Mark!!
Betty (*to Craze*) Don't just stand there, do something! / It's his wedding day.
Mark Oh! Holy shit! God help me, / please, if you're up there! I'll never swear again; I'll even start going to church.
Craze I can't help him, he wants to live.
Betty Well, think of something. It's all right for you, you're already dead.

Mark Mam! I'm too young to die.
Craze So was I.
Betty Well, you shouldn't have gone and got yourself shot should you.
Craze I didn't / do it on purpose.
Mark Never mind him, talk to me, Mam!
Betty It's all right, love. Craze is going to help you.
Mark Oh! No, not him, anyone but him.

Craze prepares himself to perform a miracle

Craze How do you think it feels to be shot with your own gun?
Betty Painful.
Mark } *(together)* { Yeh.
Craze } { By my own wife.
Betty It was Moira?
Mark Not her again.
Craze It was in the *Evening Post*.
Betty I don't get the *Evening Post*.
Mark Sod the *Evening Post*! I'll be front page headlines if somebody doesn't
  do something soon.
Craze Your neighbours are going to find this very strange.

*Mark moves effortlessly up the roof as though being pulled by some
supernatural force*

Mark Ahhh! / What's happening?

*We hears gasps from the crowd down below, as they see what appears to be
Mark miraculously moving up the roof*

Betty Be careful with him!
Mark Jesus! Oh! Jesus help me. What the hell's happening!

Craze walks back up the roof with Mark in his arms

Betty It's all right, he won't let you fall.
Craze She walked into the police station one week and two days later and
  confessed.
Betty You mean she could have got away with it?
Craze She followed me, three bullets in my back. Ruined a perfectly good
  suit.
Betty *(in wonderment, to herself)* Moira.
Mark *(talking to himself)* I know what this is, it's a pre-wedding nightmare.
  I'm going to wake up in a minute, that's it.

Craze lowers Mark back on to the roof next to the skylight

Ow! Me foot! (*He pulls down his sock to look at his swollen ankle*)

Craze She only got three years, diminished responsibility on account of her being pregnant. She married again, had another three children. She's a grandmother now.

Betty Where were you going?

Craze Nowhere ... I was meeting someone.

Betty A woman?

Craze She was a mate's girlfriend. I was giving her a message.

Betty You were having a thing with her, weren't you?

Craze (*an obvious lie*) I wasn't.

Betty Admit it?

Craze I'm telling you.

Betty You don't have to lie, Craze, you're dead.

Mark I've twisted me ankle ——

His mother takes no notice

—— if anyone's interested. (*He removes his shoe*) Mother!

Betty is suddenly aware that her son is hurt

Betty What, love?

Mark (*he inspects his painful ankle*) I said I've twisted me ankle, it's probably sprained.

Craze Tell him to go back down.

Betty You better go back down, Mark, see what your father's doing.

Mark Yeh, right! No problem ... (*Sotto voce*) It's all right, Mam, 'cos none of this is real ... (*Louder*) Tell him, thanks.

Craze It's all right, it's the least I could do.

Betty He says it's the least he could do.

Mark So what are you going to do, Mam?

Craze Tell him, I'll see him down.

Betty Craze is going to help me ... He helped you, didn't he? Trust me. It's all right. You get yourself cleaned up. Jo'll be arriving at the church any minute now.

Mark I think I'll go have a lie on my bed and see if I can wake up.

Betty Yes, that's a good idea. Get your dad to give your jacket a good brush down.

The sweeping broom appears through the skylight, and Donald follows it

As our attention is on the skylight area, Craze disappears

Donald I'm here! (*He looks to where Mark was*) Grab hold of ... where's he gone?

Mark You took your time.

A startled Donald turns to see Mark sitting at the side of the skylight

Donald How did you get there?

Betty He crawled.

Donald On your knees?

Mark Well, that's how you usually crawl.

Donald I've rung the fire brigade.

Betty I thought I told you / not to ——

Donald The police, you said, you never mentioned the fire brigade.

Betty Well, they are going to have a side show, aren't they?

Donald Not if you come down now they won't.

Betty Oh! Look there's another car.

Donald We've just got to keep her talking till the fire brigade arrive.

Betty I think it's the bridal car.

Mark Where?

Betty It is.

Donald Somebody better tell the poor lass. Shall I tell your Aunty Margaret to go?

Mark No! I'll have to do it.

Betty Her dad's opening the car door for her.

Mark I can't let her go in the church.

Betty She's going to be ever so upset.

Mark Let me get in! I've got to stop her.

Donald Go steady. They'll be here soon.

Betty Oh! She's all in white; it's down to the floor. She looks a picture.

Mark disappears down the skylight

Mark (*off*) Owww! Me foot!!

Betty Where's he gone?

Donald To tell her there isn't going to be a wedding.

Betty I'm not stopping him.

Donald You are. How can he get married with his mother on the roof?

Betty He should just do what he wants to do ... I wish I was dead.

Donald Am I that bad?

Betty (*looking for Craze*) Where's he gone?

Donald I've told you, to the church.

Betty I'll have to do it by myself now.

Donald What?

Betty Nothing.

Donald Why have you got that old dress on?

Betty Do you remember it?

Donald (*struggling to remember it*) Didn't your Margaret give you it?

Betty (*reflecting back*) That's right, that's what I told you.

Donald Come on Betty, don't be like this. It's the best time, you know.

Betty What?

Donald We'll have time to ourselves now, just you and me. We can sell this house, buy something smaller and a caravan at the coast or one of those camper vans that you like ... We could have trips out, we can go down and see our Mark and Jo in Nottingham, stay with them a couple of days ...

Betty Where did it all go?

Donald All what?

Betty I was nineteen yesterday. I'm still nineteen, Donald, you do hear what I'm saying; nineteen!

Donald Yes love, nineteen.

Betty You don't understand.

Donald I do.

Betty You don't, 'cos if you did, you wouldn't be like you are with me. I had a very strange experience last Saturday when our Mark took me to the Asda, I saw something I'd never seen before. I'd done all me fruit and veg and I was just reaching out for me cottage cheese and that's when I saw it. I was so shocked, it stopped me in me tracks. Do you know what it was I saw. It was a hand, somebody else's hand, somebody old, somebody much older than me; it had little brown spots on the back, the little finger had gone a funny shape and the skin was all sort of bunched together in little folds, making a sort of pattern but the funny thing was, this hand had my wedding ring on it. I stood there just staring at that hand and I thought who did that? Who put that hand on my arm, who swapped it when I wasn't looking, who played that trick on me. I felt hot. My heart was thumping and the sweat was trickling down my body. I wanted to run out of that store screaming.

Donald What did you do?

Betty I bought meself some rubber gloves ... I've wasted all that time.

Donald You haven't wasted it, Betty.

We hear soft music from within the loft: Johnnie Mathis's "Someone"

Betty I'm a passionate woman, Donald. I needed a passionate man.
Donald I can be passionate.
Betty No, you can't.
Donald I can. I was passionate once, I can be passionate again. You just wait there.

He goes back down

Donald (*off*) Who put the record-player on?
Craze (*off*) Me.

Craze appears from the far side of the roof, walking with ease up to the top, then along the ridge

Betty You're back, then?
Craze Do you remember this one?
Betty As if I could forget.

Craze starts to dance along the rooftop, as though he is balancing on the very ridge of the roof. He moves effortlessly along the length of the roof as he sings to her

(*During this*) You always had a lovely voice. It was your voice I fell for, I didn't stand a chance once I'd heard it.

Craze walks along so that he is very near to the chimney. Betty and Craze are bathed in a warm romantic light

You were always such a daredevil. A wild one. "Let's run away to the seaside," you'd say.
Craze I meant it.
Betty You wouldn't have gone.
Craze I would run anywhere with you, Betty. In fact, you killed me, by not coming with me.
Betty Did I really?
Craze Yes, because I was always looking after that, looking for what I had with you.
Betty Well, fancy that.
Craze My beautiful, beautiful Betty.
Betty "My beautiful, beautiful Betty," you always used to say that ...

There is a noise, off

They're coming back, Mark and Jo, they're running up the street, well our
Mark's limping.

Craze You're going to have to make your mind up.

Betty I'm not going down.

Craze Well, come on up then.

Mark (*off*) Mam!

Betty waves to Mark

Betty I'm still here! Hallo, Jo. I like your dress, you look lovely.

Mark (*off*) She wants you to come down, Mam!

*We hear fire engine sirens. They grow louder throughout the following
dialogue*

Betty It's all go, isn't it?

Mark (*off*) Jo wants to talk to you, Mam.

Betty (*shouting over the top of the fire engines*) Well, she'll have to shout.

Mark (*off*) Can we come up?

Betty If you want.

*Blue lights flicker from below. There is the screech of brakes. The sirens stop.
From within the loft the record on the record-player is stuck*

Betty Will somebody turn that damn thing off. (*Shouting to the audience*)
Are you having a good time, Mrs Cooper? Beats the television any day!
Think of all the gossiping you can do. It's nearly over and then you can go
back in your little houses and say, "Fancy all them years we lived over the
road from her and we never knew she was mad". Only I'm not mad, I've
never felt so sane in my life. It could be you on this roof! Think about it,
Mrs Cooper!

Craze They're coming up for you, Betty!

Betty They can do what they like.

Fireman's voice (*off, over a tannoy*) We'd like you to keep perfectly still,
Mrs Derbyshire. Chief Fire Officer John Barlow will be coming up on the
crane to assist you off the roof.

Betty Very nice but I don't need any "assistance" thank you. Haven't you
got anything better to do, a fire to put out or something?

The broken record stops

Craze (*holding out his hand to Betty*) It's time, Betty.

*Betty takes hold of Craze's hand. Gasps again from down below as she walks
up the roof to the top*

> *Mark appears at the opening to the skylight*

Mark Mam! What are you doing?
Betty Going higher.
Mark But, Mam!

*As Craze helps Betty to the very top of the roof, we hear Donald's voice, even
higher*

Donald (*off*) Betty!

Betty, Mark and Craze look up. Gasps from the crowds

Betty I don't believe it.
Mark Oh! My God!

> *The basket and bottom of a large multi-coloured hot air balloon come into
> sight from above, containing Donald*

Betty I don't believe it.
Mark Where did you get that from?
Donald (*referring to their earlier conversation*) Never you mind. It's not
what you say in this life, Mark, it's what you do.
Mark This is going from bad to worse.

> *Mark goes down*

Betty I don't believe it.
Donald Well, you better do, 'cos it's real enough.
Betty (*moved*) Aw! Donald, what a thing to do.
Donald It was supposed to be for after the wedding, I've been planning it for
weeks. You've been going on about it since your Margaret's fiftieth, so I
thought, "What the hell, it'll be a surprise for her", so I booked it.
Betty You've never done anything like this before.
Donald Ah! Well, you see it's all going to be different from now on.
Betty Is it really?
Donald Oh! Yes. We've got a new life ahead of us, Betty. It's you and me
now. Is this passionate enough for you, do you think?

Betty It's very romantic, Donald.
Donald It cost me a fortune.
Betty Don't spoil it.
Donald I'm not complaining, it's worth every penny.

He operates the balloon so that it moves over towards her

Come with me.
Craze Don't do it, Betty.
Betty (*to herself*) Why not?
Donald That's right.
Craze It's only a balloon ... (*he clicks his fingers*) and it's gone.
Betty (*to herself*) And what are we left with?
Donald It's an experience! You said it.
Betty Did I?
Donald Don't you remember?
Betty Oh! Yes, so I did.
Donald Well then?
Craze Well then what?
Betty (*answering Craze*) I don't know.

The balloon hovers over the roof top

Donald Come on, Betty, we'll fly together.
Betty Where to?
Donald Anywhere.
Craze He can't change, he's too old.
Betty Anywhere?
Donald That's right, anywhere you like.
Craze It's finished.
Donald Anywhere you want ... (*Shouting to break her daze*) Betty!
Betty Yes, that's me.
Donald I said we can go anywhere ——

He is drowned out by the fireman

Fireman's voice (*off, over tannoy*) Mr and Mrs Derbyshire, will you both keep still / and listen very carefully to my instructions.
Donald Ignore him! I know what I'm doing.
Fireman (*off*) It's very important that you / fasten the belt ...
Donald The only thing that's important is you and me, Betty.
Fireman (*off*) We'll line / the cage up with the roof so that you'll be able to step straight into it.
Donald Did you hear what I said? (*Holding out his hand to her and shouting*

over the top of the fireman's voice) Betty! ... Grab hold of my hand ... I won't let you fall .... I've got it nice and steady ... Come on, love. Come on.

Betty is just about to raise her hand to Donald when a fireman's crane and cradle come up from the side of the house towards the chimney. Mark is in the cradle

Mark Mam!
Donald (*seeing Mark*) Oh! No! What you doing?
Mark I've come to bring her down.
Donald (*he was handling this*) It's all right, I've got her.
Mark No, she's getting in here.
Donald She's coming with me.
Mark (*warning*) Dad! Let's just get her down off this roof, shall we.
Donald Why do you always have to interfere?
Craze Say "goodbye" to them, Betty.
Mark Just step on to this, Mam, and you'll be safe.
Craze You've been safe all your life, Betty. It's time to go.
Mark If we hurry up I'll still be able to get married.
Donald (*reaching out to her*) Come on, Betty, you can do it.
Craze My beautiful, beautiful Betty.
Mark Come on, Mam.
Donald Trust me.
Craze You wanted me here ...
Mark Mam!
Craze Remember how desperate you were?
Donald I was passionate once ...
Mark We love you, Mam ...
Craze You pleaded with me ——
Donald I can be passionate again ...
Mark Jo's waiting for us ...
Craze —— "Take me with you," you said.
Mark It's her day.
Betty (*at the top of her voice, with great gusto*) But it's my moment! (*Matter of factly*) Get your father out of that balloon.
Mark What?
Betty (*shouting down to the fireman*) Send your machine to get my husband or I'll jump off the other side.
Donald Betty!
Betty I mean it and I don't want to hear any more ...
Craze (*questioning*) Betty?
Betty I've decided! Did you hear me down there? Send your machine over!

The red arm of the crane goes over to meet the balloon

Donald Now what?
Betty Now get on that thing with our Mark!
Donald And what about the balloon?
Betty Never mind the balloon, just do as I say for once in your life.
Mark (*passing his father the safety harness*) Here, put that round you.
Donald What the ... / I got the ——
Mark Just do it, Dad.

Donald fastens the harness round him

Donald I don't know what she thinks she's playing at.
Betty You said I could go anywhere I liked, Donald ——
Donald I said we / could go ——
Betty — and Mark said I could do anything I liked ——
Mark (*not sure what she's got planned*) That's right.
Betty Well, I've picked what I want to do and I've picked where I want to go, so there you are.
Mark (*trying to humour her*) Well, that's good, at least we're making progress.
Donald So what am I supposed to do now?
Betty Get in that thing with our Mark.
Donald And then what?
Mark Don't panic, Dad. She's right, let's just get you down and then we can sort me mam out.
Donald I hope you know what you're doing.

Donald steps on to the cradle. Gasps and chattering from down below

Betty (*shouting to the fireman as she grabs hold of the basket*) Right! They're ready!
Mark What y'doing?
Betty Holding on.

The cradle moves Mark and Donald slightly away from the roof top

Mark Don't do anything stupid, Mam.
Betty I wouldn't dream of it.

Muttering from the neighbours swells as Betty starts to hoist her skirts to get into the balloon

Mark			Jesus Christ!
Donald	*(together)*		For God's sake be careful.
Craze			What do you think you're doing, Betty?
Fireman			*(off)* Mrs Derbyshire, do not get into the balloon. I repeat, do not get into the balloon. Mrs Derbyshire, I have to warn you that ——

Betty Oh shut up!!

She lifts her hand up to fire the burner

Mark You'll kill yourself, Mam.
Betty Well, if I do, I'll die happy.

As the balloon begins to ascend, we hear the church bells start to peal, calling the bride and groom to their wedding service

Donald Betty!
Mark I'm going to wake / up in a minute.
Donald She's having a nervous breakdown.
Mark Mam!
Craze I'll catch you later.
Betty Yes, you do that and do you know what?

Craze		
Mark	*(together)* What?	
Donald		

Betty *(to Craze)* I'd have shot you too. You should have stayed in my head, you were all right there ——
Donald Who's she talking ——
Mark Who do y'think? (*He shouts*) Jo!

Jo appears in the skylight

Betty *(to Mark)* Go and get married, Mark! They'll all be there waiting. And Jo! You make a lovely bride. I'm sorry about the delay, love, but I've had a lot to work out. You know I think you've got it right, so make each other happy. Donald, it was a lovely gesture, love, but it was too late. Bye, Mrs Cooper! Mr Cooper! Margaret! Mal! Everyone! D'you know something, we've got to live this life for every moment because this might be all we've got.

The Lights go down on Mark and Donald standing in the fireman's cradle,

Jo, in her bridal wear, framed in the skylight and Craze still standing on the roof top. The wedding bells are still chiming. We hear the fading voice of Betty happily singing the Nimble advertisement theme as she flies through the air

Black-out

FURNITURE AND PROPERTY LIST

Further dressing may be added at the director's discretion

ACT I

On stage: Artificial Christmas tree
Box containing baubles, old Christmas cards and rope
Brown carrier-bag containing old Christmas cards
Used tins of paint
Old-fashioned heavy 50s style record-player
Box containing old LPs. *In one of the LP sleeves:* letter
Rolled-up carpet
Lilac wooden high-chair
Parts of a baby's wooden cot
Water-tank
Three battered suitcases; one of them large and brown, containing clothes, **Betty**'s yellow fifties dress, etc.
Four dining-room chairs
Cabinet covered in papers
Trunk containing underskirts, etc.
Rolls of linoleum

Off stage: Broom (**Betty**)

Personal: **Betty**: wedding outfit accessories (handbag, etc.), hat pin
Mark: watch

ACT II

Set: Dining-room chair under skylight
Open skylight slightly

Off stage: Ladder (**Donald**)

Personal: **Mark**: watch
Donald: watch, handkerchief

LIGHTING PLOT

Practical fittings required: loft light, operated by cord

1 interior, 1 exterior

ACT I

To open:	Small amount of daylight filtering through skylight	
Cue 1	The flap opens *Shaft of light from landing below streams up into loft*	(Page 1)
Cue 2	**Betty** pulls light cord *Full stage lighting as loft light comes on*	(Page 2)
Cue 3	**Betty** dances and the skirt of her dress swirls *Lights change and glitter ball descends to represent a dance hall of the late fifties*	(Page 18)
Cue 4	The loft flap opens with a bang *All dance hall effects cease: lights snap to previous state*	(Page 18)
Cue 5	**Craze** pulls **Betty** down to his side *Lights change to reflect an evening in the park*	(Page 28)
Cue 6	**Betty** and **Craze** kiss *Lights fade to black-out*	(Page 29)

ACT II

To open:	Full stage lighting; loft light on; a bit more sunlight from skylight	
Cue 7	The stage half rotates to reveal a section of the roof *Adjust lights accordingly*	(Page 37)
Cue 8	The stage rotates to fully reveal roof, loft disappears *Adjust lights accordingly*	(Page 39)
Cue 9	**Craze** walks along to near the chimney *Bathe **Betty** and **Craze** in warm romantic lighting*	(Page 49)
Cue 10	**Betty**: "If you want." *Blue lights flicker from below roof*	(Page 50)
Cue 11	**Betty**: " ... this might be all we've got." *Lights fade down to black-out as Betty disappears*	(Page 56)

EFFECTS PLOT

ACT I

Cue 1   The broom disappears from flap   (Page 1)
           Sound of heavy books being placed on top of another

Cue 2   **Betty** puts record on   (Page 16)
           Music plays : The Platters, "Twilight Time"

Cue 3   **Betty** takes record off   (Page 16)
           Music ceases

Cue 4   **Betty** puts record on   (Page 18)
           Johnny Mathis song plays

Cue 5   The loft flap opens with a bang   (Page 18)
           Music ceases

ACT II

Note: Margaret's lines and the gasps and chatter from below the roof are not given here as cues, since they can be performed live by the backstage crew, etc.

Cue 6	**Betty**: " ... we're too old to change so ——" *Loud crack from gutter and creaks as it gives slightly*	(Page 43)
Cue 7	**Betty**: " ... scraggy-haired daughter." *Another crack from gutter*	(Page 44)
Cue 8	**Donald**: "You haven't wasted it, Betty." *Johnnie Mathis's "Someone" plays from loft*	(Page 48)
Cue 9	**Betty**: " ... you always used to say that ..." *Noise, off, to indicate arrival of Mark and Jo*	(Page 49)
Cue 10	**Mark**: "She wants you to come down, Mam!" *Fire engine sirens*	(Page 50)
Cue 11	**Betty**: "If you want." *Screech of breaks, sirens cease, record gets stuck*	(Page 50)
Cue 12	**Betty**: " ... a fire to put out or something?" *Broken record ceases*	(Page 50)
Cue 13	**Donald**: "I said we can go anywhere ——" *Fireman's voice over tannoy as per script, pp. 52 — 53*	(Page 52)
Cue 14	**Betty** gets into the balloon *Fireman's voice over tannoy as per script, p. 55*	(Page 55)
Cue 15	The balloon begins to ascend *Church bells start to peal until end of play*	(Page 55)